BUBBLE TEA

BUBBLE TEA

RECIPES AND PHOTOGRAPHY BY SANDRA MAHUT
ILLUSTRATIONS BY VALENTINE FERRANDI

CONTENTS

32 CRÈME BRÛLÉE	**36** JASMINE GREEN TEA WITH LIME	**38** GREEN APPLE
40 PASSIONFRUIT	**42** POMEGRANATE AND GRENADINE	**46** RASPBERRY
48 LYCHEE AND ROSE SYRUP	**50** STRAWBERRY JELLY ICED TEA	**54** GRAPEFRUIT JELLY
56 LEMON JELLY	**58** GRASSY JELLY WITH COCONUT MILK	**60** PANDAN JELLY

INGREDIENTS

Ice cubes

Tea (green, black, white)

Milk (cow's milk or plantbased)

Sugar or fruit syrup

Tapioca pearls, jelly or fruit

BEST SERVED

Bubble tea is prepared in 15 minutes and can be enjoyed instantly.

Tapioca or fruit pearls can be kept for several days in a sweet syrup.

TOOLS TO HAVE

1 XXL straw
1 measuring spoon or scale
1 shaker
1 thermos
1 measuring jug or 200–400 ml
(7–13½ fl oz) jigger
2 tall glasses

Bubble tea
TUTORIAL
IN 4 STEPS

1 Prepare the tea.

2 Combine and shake.

3 Add the pearls, jelly or fruit.

4 Add straw and sip.

FUN FACTS

Bubble tea is the favourite drink in **Taiwan**!

•

The **XXL straw** is the essential element
for sucking up the pearls!

•

Bubble tea was born on the streets of Taiwan
in the 1980s!
The drink is hydrating, but also filling! It easily replaces
dessert when eating street food.

Orgeat and almond milk

FOR 2 PEOPLE

PREP 15 MINUTES

400 ml (13½ fl oz) boiling water

10 g (¼ oz) Assam black tea

300 ml (10 fl oz) almond milk

100 ml (3½ fl oz) orgeat syrup

160 g (5½ oz) cooked Tapioca pearls (page 44)

 PREPARE THE TEA

In a teapot, pour the boiling water over the black tea and leave to steep for 10 minutes.
Strain and pour the tea into a thermos to keep it warm.

 COMBINE AND SHAKE

In a shaker, combine the hot tea, almond milk and orgeat syrup. Shake two or three times.

 ADD TAPIOCA PEARLS

Place the tapioca pearls at the bottom of each glass and pour over the tea.

 ADD STRAW AND SIP AWAY

Add the XXL straw and enjoy.

Hot coconut latte

FOR 2 PEOPLE

PREP 15 MINUTES

400 ml (13½ fl oz) boiling
water

10 g (¼ oz) Assam
black tea

100 ml (3½ fl oz) coconut
syrup

300 ml (10 fl oz) coconut
milk

160 g (5½ oz) cooked
tapioca pearls (page 44)

 1 PREPARE THE TEA

In a teapot, pour the boiling water over the black tea
and leave to steep for 10 minutes.
    Strain and pour the tea into a thermos to keep
it warm.

 2 COMBINE AND SHAKE

Pour the hot tea into a shaker and add the coconut syrup
and coconut milk. Shake two or three times.

 3 ADD TAPIOCA PEARLS

Place the tapioca pearls at the bottom of each glass
and pour over the tea.

 4 ADD STRAW AND SIP AWAY

Add the XXL straw and enjoy hot. This tea can also
be enjoyed cold in the summer.

Peach and oat milk

FOR 2 PEOPLE
PREP 15 MINUTES

400 ml (13½ fl oz) boiling water

10 g (¼ oz) Assam black tea

100 ml (3½ fl oz) peach syrup

300 ml (10 fl oz) oat milk

160 g (5½ oz) cooked Tapioca pearls (page 44)

 PREPARE THE TEA

In a teapot, pour the boiling water over the black tea and leave to steep for 10 minutes.

Strain and pour the tea into a thermos to keep it warm or a carafe to allow to cool.

 COMBINE AND SHAKE

Pour the warm or cold tea into a shaker then add the peach syrup and oat milk. Shake two or three times.

 ADD TAPIOCA PEARLS

Place the tapioca pearls at the bottom of each glass and pour over the tea.

 ADD STRAW AND SIP AWAY

Add the XXL straw and drink hot or cold.

Caramel latte

FOR 2 PEOPLE	
PREP 15 MINUTES	

400 ml (13½ fl oz) boiling water

10 g (¼ oz) Assam black tea

100 ml (3½ fl oz) caramel syrup

2 tablespoons vanilla syrup

300 ml (10 fl oz) full-cream (whole) milk

160 g (5½ oz) cooked Tapioca pearls (page 44)

1 PREPARE THE TEA

In a teapot, pour the boiling water over the black tea and leave to steep for 10 minutes.
Strain and pour the tea into a thermos to keep it warm.

2 COMBINE AND SHAKE

Pour the hot tea into a shaker, add the caramel and vanilla syrups, then add the milk. Shake two or three times so that the syrup and tea has combined.

3 ADD TAPIOCA PEARLS

Place the tapioca pearls at the bottom of each glass and pour over the tea.

4 ADD STRAW AND SIP AWAY

Add the XXL straw and enjoy hot. This tea can also be enjoyed cold in the summer.

Strawberry banana

FOR 2 PEOPLE

PREP 15 MINUTES

400 ml (13½ fl oz) boiling water

10 g (¼ oz) Assam black tea

100 ml (3½ fl oz) strawberry-banana syrup

300 ml (10 fl oz) plantbased milk of your choice

160 g (5½ oz) cooked Tapioca pearls (page 44)

strawberries, to garnish

 PREPARE THE TEA

In a teapot, pour the boiling water over the black tea and leave to steep for 10 minutes.

Strain and pour the tea into a thermos to keep it warm.

 COMBINE AND SHAKE

Pour the hot tea into a shaker, add the strawberry-banana syrup and the plantbased milk. Shake two or three times.

 ADD TAPIOCA PEARLS

Place the tapioca pearls and a few slices of fresh strawberry at the bottom of each glass and pour over the tea.

 ADD STRAW AND SIP AWAY

Add the XXL straw and enjoy hot. This tea can also be enjoyed cold in the summer.

Mango and passionfruit

FOR 2 PEOPLE

PREP 15 MINUTES

400 ml (13½ fl oz) boiling water

10 g (¼ oz) Assam black tea

1 passionfruit, cut in half

100 ml (3½ fl oz) mango or tropical-flavoured syrup

300 ml (10 fl oz) plantbased or full-cream (whole) milk

160 g (5½ oz) cooked Tapioca pearls (page 44)

a few ice cubes and 2 slices of mango, to garnish (optional)

 PREPARE THE TEA

In a teapot, pour the boiling water over the black tea and leave to steep for 10 minutes.

Strain and pour the tea into a carafe to cool, or into a thermos if drinking warm.

 COMBINE AND SHAKE

Place the passionfruit pulp in a small colander, strain the juice and discard the seeds and pulp. Pour the passionfruit juice into a shaker, add the tea, mango syrup and milk. Shake two or three times.

 ADD TAPIOCA PEARLS

Place the tapioca pearls at the bottom of each glass and pour over the tea.

 ADD STRAW AND SIP AWAY

Add ice cubes (if drinking cold), garnish with a slice of mango, add the XXL straw and enjoy.

Brown sugar

FOR 2 PEOPLE

PREP 15 MINUTES

400 ml (13½ fl oz) boiling
water

10 g (¼ oz) Assam
black tea

100 ml (3½ fl oz) brown
sugar syrup, plus extra
to finish

300 ml (10 fl oz) full-cream
(whole) milk

160 g (5½ oz) cooked
Tapioca pearls (page 44)

1 PREPARE THE TEA

In a teapot, pour the boiling water over the black tea and leave to steep for 10 minutes.
 Strain and pour the tea into a thermos to keep it warm.

2 COMBINE AND SHAKE

Pour the hot tea into a shaker, add the brown sugar syrup and the milk. Shake two or three times.

3 ADD TAPIOCA PEARLS

In each glass, place tapioca pearls, sprinkle the sides of the glasses with extra brown sugar syrup and pour over the tea. It can be enjoyed hot, warm or cold.

4 ADD STRAW AND SIP AWAY

Add the XXL straw and enjoy immediately.

Matcha tea

FOR 2 PEOPLE
PREP 15 MINUTES

10 g (¼ oz) matcha tea powder

300 ml (10 fl oz) hot water

160 g (5½ oz) cooked Tapioca pearls (page 44)

300 ml (10 fl oz) plantbased or full-cream (whole) milk

80 ml (⅓ cup) sugar syrup

a few ice cubes

 PREPARE THE TEA

In a bowl, combine the matcha tea and 50 ml (1¾ fl oz) of the hot water. Whisk with a bamboo whisk or mini whisk, then pour into the teapot and add the rest of the water.

 ADD THE TAPIOCA PEARLS

Place the tapioca pearls at the bottom of each glass, then pour over the milk and sugar syrup.

 POUR THE TEA

Pour over the matcha tea.

 ADD STRAW AND SIP AWAY

Add ice cubes and the XXL straw and enjoy.

Condensed milk, cream and vanilla

FOR 2 PEOPLE

PREP 15 MINUTES

450 ml (15 fl oz) boiling water

10 g (¼ oz) Assam black tea

160 g (5½ oz) cooked Tapioca pearls (page 44)

200 ml (7 fl oz) sweetened condensed milk

2 tablespoons vanilla syrup

ready-to-use whipped cream, to top

2 tablespoons brown sugar syrup

PREPARE THE TEA

In a teapot, pour the boiling water over the black tea and leave to steep for 10 minutes.

Strain and pour the tea into a thermos to keep it warm.

ADD TAPIOCA PEARLS AND COMBINE

Place the tapioca pearls at the bottom of each glass, then pour in the sweetened condensed milk and vanilla syrup. Pour in the still-hot black tea and mix with a spoon, stirring just once or twice.

ADD CREAM

Add a little whipped cream to each glass, then the brown sugar syrup.

ADD STRAW AND SIP AWAY

Add the XXL straw and enjoy immediately.

Taro

FOR 2 PEOPLE

PREP 15 MINUTES

450 ml (15 fl oz) boiling
water

10 g (¼ oz) Assam
black tea

100 ml (3½ fl oz)
sweetened condensed milk

2 tablespoons taro powder
for bubble tea

160 g (5½ oz) cooked
Tapioca pearls (page 44)

1 PREPARE THE TEA

In a teapot, pour the boiling water over the black tea and leave to steep for 10 minutes.
Strain and pour the tea into a thermos to keep it warm.

2 COMBINE AND SHAKE

Pour the hot tea into a shaker, then add the sweetened condensed milk and taro powder. Shake two or three times.

3 ADD TAPIOCA PEARLS

Place the tapioca pearls at the bottom of each glass and pour over the tea.

4 ADD STRAW AND SIP AWAY

Add the XXL straw and enjoy hot or cold.

crème brûlée

FOR 2 PEOPLE
PREP 15 MINUTES

450 ml (15 fl oz) boiling water

10 g (¼ oz) Assam black tea

160 g (5½ oz) cooked Tapioca pearls (page 44)

170 ml (⅔ cup) full-cream (whole) milk

4 teaspoons brown sugar

200 ml (7 fl oz) cream

2–3 tablespoons icing (confectioners') sugar

1 PREPARE THE TEA

In a teapot, pour the boiling water over the black tea and leave to steep for 10 minutes.

Strain and pour the tea into a thermos to keep it warm.

2 ADD TAPIOCA PEARLS AND COMBINE

In each glass, place tapioca pearls, then pour over the black tea.

In a shaker, combine the milk and a little brown sugar. Shake two or three times and pour into the glasses.

3 ADD CREAM

Whip the cream for 5 minutes with an electric whisk, add a little icing sugar and stop just before the cream becomes fully whipped. It should be thickened but not stiff.

Add it to each glass and sprinkle with brown sugar. Pass a crème brûlée torch for 4–5 seconds over the sugar.

4 ADD STRAW AND SIP AWAY

Add the XXL straw and enjoy immediately.

Bubble tea

Noun

Zenzou in Chinese, which literally translates to 'pearl milk tea', is a drink of Taiwanese origin, which appeared in the 1980s in a tea house in the city of Taichung. Bubble tea is a mixture of tea (green, black or white), cold or hot, and milk with tapioca pearls, fruit or jelly. A fruity flavour is often added, and the whole thing is consumed through a straw!

Jasmine green tea with lime

FOR 2 PEOPLE

PREP 15 MINUTES

450 ml (15 fl oz) boiling water

10 g (¼ oz) jasmine or sencha green tea

50 ml (1¾ fl oz) lime syrup

150 g (5½ oz) store-bought lime pearls

a few ice cubes

1 lime, sliced

 PREPARE THE TEA

In a teapot, pour the boiling water over the tea and leave to infuse for 10 minutes.
Strain and pour the tea into a carafe to cool.

 COMBINE AND SHAKE

In a shaker, combine the tea with the lime syrup. Shake two or three times.

 ADD FRUIT PEARLS

In each glass, place the lime pearls and a few ice cubes, then pour over the tea.

 ADD STRAW AND SIP AWAY

Add a few slices of lime, the XXL straw and enjoy very cold.

Green apple

FOR 2 PEOPLE

PREP 15 MINUTES

450 ml (15 fl oz) boiling water

10 g (¼ oz) green tea

100 ml (3½ fl oz) green apple syrup

160 g (5½ oz) store-bought green apple pearls

a few ice cubes

 1 PREPARE THE TEA

In a teapot, pour the boiling water over the green tea and leave to infuse for 10 minutes.
Strain and pour the tea into a carafe to cool.

 2 COMBINE AND SHAKE

In a shaker, combine the green tea with the green apple syrup. Shake two or three times.

 3 ADD FRUIT PEARLS

In each glass, place the green apple pearls and a few ice cubes, then pour over the tea.

 4 ADD STRAW AND SIP AWAY

Add the XXL straw and enjoy immediately.

Passionfruit

FOR 2 PEOPLE

PREP 15 MINUTES

450 ml (15 fl oz) boiling
water

10 g (¼ oz) black, green or
white tea

80 ml (⅓ cup) tropical
fruit syrup

160 g (5½ oz) store-bought
passionfruit pearls

a few ice cubes

1. PREPARE THE TEA

In a teapot, pour the boiling water over the tea and leave to infuse for 10 minutes.

Strain and pour the tea into a carafe or jug to cool.

2. COMBINE AND SHAKE

In a shaker, combine the cool tea with the tropical fruit syrup. Shake two or three times to combine.

3. ADD THE FRUIT PEARLS

In each glass, place the passionfruit pearls and a few ice cubes, then pour over the tea.

4. ADD STRAW AND SIP AWAY

Add the XXL straw and enjoy immediately.

Pomegranate and grenadine

FOR 2 PEOPLE

PREP 15 MINUTES

450 ml (15 fl oz) boiling water

10 g (¼ oz) green tea

80 ml (⅓ cup) grenadine syrup

160 g (5½ oz) store-bought pomegranate pearls

a few ice cubes

 PREPARE THE TEA

In a teapot, pour the boiling water over the green tea and leave to infuse for 10 minutes.
    Strain and pour the tea into a carafe to cool.

 COMBINE AND SHAKE

In a shaker, combine the green tea with the grenadine syrup. Shake two or three times.

 ADD FRUIT PEARLS

In each glass, place the pomegranate pearls and a few ice cubes, then pour over the tea.

 ADD STRAW AND SIP AWAY

Add the XXL straw and enjoy.

TAPIOCA PEARLS

Called 'bobas', these pearls come from bitter cassava roots. They have little taste but a very sought-after soft texture. Originating in South America, tapioca was discovered by Europeans in the 16th century. It then spread to the rest of the world and is used today in different ways.

One of the advantages of tapioca, beyond its nutritional characteristics (as an appetite suppressant), is that it is gluten-free.

FOR 2 PEOPLE

600 ml (20½ fl oz) water • 200 g (7 oz) tapioca pearls • 150 g (5½ oz) sugar

Bring 400 ml (13½ fl oz) of the water to the boil and add the tapioca pearls. Once they rise to the surface, let them cook for 30 minutes. When the 30 minutes is almost up, in a separate saucepan boil the remaining water and add the sugar, stirring until it dissolves. Once time is up for the pearls, remove them from the water with a slotted spoon and place them in the sweet syrup. They can be stored for up to 3 days in this syrup in the refrigerator.

THE PEARLS

JELLY

Fruit jelly, which can be made at home, can replace tapioca or fruit pearls in your bubble tea. You can add your favourite flavours to make the jelly you need.

FOR 2 PEOPLE

500 ml (2 cups) water, coconut water or fruit juice • 70 g (2½ oz) caster (superfine) sugar • 5 g (⅛ oz) agar-agar • 2–4 drops food colouring of your choice (red, green, yellow) or pandan flavour (green)

Bring the water and sugar to the boil. Remove the pan from the heat, add the agar-agar and mix well. Return the mixture to low heat and stir for 5 minutes.

Add a drop of food colouring and stir well to combine. Pour the mixture into a rectangular gratin dish or a plastic container. Let cool before refrigerating for 5 hours to set. Once the jelly has set, you can cut it into cubes and put it in glasses to serve.

FRUIT SYRUP PEARLS

These can be found on the shelves of supermarkets, Asian grocery stores or online on websites specialising in bubble tea. Made with a fruit-flavoured coulis, they are coated in a thin film of edible gelatine that is easily pierced when bitten.

Raspberry

FOR 2 PEOPLE

PREP 15 MINUTES

450 ml (15 fl oz) boiling water

10 g (¼ oz) green tea

60 ml (¼ cup) raspberry syrup

160 g (5½ oz) store-bought raspberry pearls

a few ice cubes

4–6 fresh raspberries

1 PREPARE THE TEA

In a teapot, pour the boiling water over the green tea and leave to infuse for 10 minutes. Strain and pour the tea into a carafe to cool.

2 COMBINE AND SHAKE

In a shaker, combine the cold green tea with the raspberry syrup. Shake two or three times to combine.

3 ADD FRUIT PEARLS

In each glass, place the raspberry pearls and a few ice cubes, then pour over the tea.

4 ADD STRAW AND SIP AWAY

Add the XXL straw, a few raspberries and enjoy.

Lychee and rose syrup

FOR 2 PEOPLE

PREP 15 MINUTES

450 ml (15 fl oz) boiling water

10 g (¼ oz) white tea

80 ml (⅓ cup) lychee juice

160 g (5½ oz) store-bought lychee pearls

a few ice cubes

50 ml (1¾ fl oz) rose syrup

 PREPARE THE TEA

In a teapot, pour the boiling water over the white tea and leave to infuse for 10 minutes.
Strain and pour the tea into a carafe to cool.

 COMBINE AND SHAKE

In a shaker, combine the white tea with the lychee juice. Shake two or three times.

 ADD FRUIT PEARLS

In each glass, place the lychee pearls and a few ice cubes, then pour over the tea.

 ADD STRAW AND SIP AWAY

Add the XXL straw and pour in the rose syrup at the last moment (this gives a gradient effect).

Strawberry jelly iced tea

FOR 2 PEOPLE

PREP 15 MINUTES

450 ml (15 fl oz) boiling water

10 g (¼ oz) green tea

80 ml (⅓ cup) peach syrup

80 g (2¾ oz) strawberry jelly (see page 45)

a few ice cubes

4 strawberries, sliced

 PREPARE THE TEA

In a teapot, pour the boiling water over the green tea and leave to infuse for 10 minutes.
Strain and pour the tea into a carafe to cool.

 COMBINE AND SHAKE

In a shaker, combine the green tea with the peach syrup. Shake two or three times.

 ADD FRUIT JELLY

In each glass, place the strawberry jelly and a few ice cubes, then pour over the tea.

④ **ADD STRAW AND SIP AWAY**

Add the XXL straw, a few strawberry slices and enjoy immediately.

THE GOLDEN RULES

For a 400 ml (13½ fl oz) serve
To enjoy with or without ice cubes

FOR A STRONG BUBBLE TEA

80 g (2¾ oz) pearls

150 ml (5 fl oz) milk

200 ml (7 fl oz) tea

50 ml (1¾ fl oz) syrup

FOR A SWEETER, LESS MILKY BUBBLE TEA

80 g (2¾ oz) pearls

100 ml (3½ fl oz) milk

200 ml (7 fl oz) tea

100 ml (3½ fl oz) syrup

FOR A MILKIER, LESS SWEET BUBBLE TEA

80 g (2¾ oz) pearls

180 ml (6 fl oz) milk

200 ml (7 fl oz) tea

20 ml (¾ fl oz) syrup

FOR A BUBBLE TEA WITH LOTS OF PEARLS

120 g (4½ oz) pearls

50 ml (1¾ fl oz) syrup

200 ml (7 fl oz) tea

150 ml (5 fl oz) milk

Grapefruit jelly

FOR 2 PEOPLE

PREP 15 MINUTES

450 ml (15 fl oz) boiling water

10 g (¼ oz) white tea

80 ml (⅓ cup) freshly squeezed grapefruit juice

1 tablespoon caster (superfine) sugar or sugar syrup

150 g (5½ oz) grapefruit jelly (see page 45)

a few slices of grapefruit (optional)

 PREPARE THE TEA

In a teapot, pour the boiling water over the white tea and leave to infuse for 10 minutes.
Strain and pour the tea into a carafe to cool.

 COMBINE AND SHAKE

In a shaker, combine the tea, grapefruit juice and sugar. Shake two or three times.

 ADD FRUIT JELLY

In each glass, place the fruit jelly, then pour over the tea.

4 **ADD STRAW AND SIP AWAY**

Add the XXL straw and enjoy immediately. Add a few grapefruit slices to the glass, if you like.

Lemon jelly

FOR 2 PEOPLE	
PREP 15 MINUTES	

450 ml (15 fl oz) boiling
water

10 g (¼ oz) white tea

80 ml (⅓ cup) lemon juice

1 tablespoon caster
(superfine) sugar or
sugar syrup

150 g (5½ oz) lemon jelly
(see page 45)

a few slices of lemon
(optional)

1 PREPARE THE TEA

In a teapot, pour the boiling water over the white tea and leave to infuse for 10 minutes.

Strain and pour the tea into a carafe or jug then allow to cool.

2 COMBINE AND SHAKE

In a shaker, combine the tea, lemon juice and sugar. Shake two or three times, so that the sugar has slightly disolved.

3 ADD FRUIT JELLY

In each glass, place the lemon jelly, then pour over the tea.

4 ADD STRAW AND SIP AWAY

Add the XXL straw and enjoy immediately. You can add a slice of lemon to the glass, if you like

Grassy jelly with coconut milk

FOR 2 PEOPLE

PREP 15 MINUTES

450 ml (15 fl oz) boiling water

10 g (¼ oz) green tea

200 ml (7 fl oz) coconut milk

150 g (5½ oz) grass (herb) jelly (see page 45)

a few ice cubes

50 ml (1¾ fl oz) cherry syrup

 PREPARE THE TEA

In a teapot, pour the boiling water over the green tea and leave to infuse for 10 minutes.
Strain and pour the tea into a carafe to cool.

 COMBINE AND SHAKE

In a shaker, combine the green tea and coconut milk. Shake two or three times.

 ADD THE GRASS JELLY

Cut the grass jelly into small cubes and add to each glass. Pour over the tea mixture and add ice cubes.

 ADD STRAW AND SIP AWAY

Add the XXL straw, pour in the cherry syrup and mix with the straw before tasting.

Pandan jelly

FOR 2 PEOPLE

PREP 15 MINUTES

450 ml (15 fl oz) boiling water

10 g (¼ oz) white tea

100 ml (3½ fl oz) aloe vera juice

1 tablespoon caster (superfine) sugar or sugar syrup

150 g (5½ oz) pandan jelly (see page 45)

a few ice cubes

1 **PREPARE THE TEA**

In a teapot, pour the boiling water over the white tea and leave to infuse for 10 minutes.
Strain and pour the tea into a carafe to cool.

2 **COMBINE AND SHAKE**

In a shaker, combine the tea, aloe vera juice and sugar. Shake two or three times.

3 **ADD FRUIT JELLY**

In each glass, place the pandan jelly, then pour over the tea.

4 **ADD STRAW AND SIP AWAY**

Add the XXL straw and a few ice cubes before tasting.

Waffle lollipops

200 g (7 oz) semi-salted butter • 200 ml (7 fl oz) milk • 22 g (¾ oz) fresh baker's yeast or 7 g (¼ oz) instant dry baker's yeast • 500 g (3⅓ cups) '00' flour • 40 g (1½ oz) brown sugar • 2 eggs • sticks for the lollipops • ready-whipped cream • 150 g (5½ oz) sprinkles

Take out the butter 2 hours before preparing the dough to soften it.
Warm the milk, put it in the bowl of a food processor and add the yeast.

Add the flour, brown sugar and eggs. Knead for 5 minutes on the slowest speed. Add the soft butter and knead on low speed for 10 minutes. Gather the dough into a ball in the centre of the bowl and cover the bowl. Leave the dough to rise at room temperature for 1 hour 30 minutes. Take 100 g (3½ oz) portions and cook them in a waffle iron.

Insert a stick in each waffle and enjoy warm with a little whipped cream and some sprinkles.

OR ALSO WITH

coconut balls
and fruit

First published in France by Hachette Livre (Marabout) in 2023
Hachette Book 58, rue Jean-Bleuzen 92178 Vanves Cedex

This edition published in 2024 by Smith Street Books
Naarm (Melbourne) | Australia
smithstreetbooks.com

ISBN: 978-1-9227-5498-1

Smith Street Books respectfully acknowledges the Wurundjeri People of the Kulin Nation, who are the Traditional Owners of the land on which we work, and we pay our respects to their Elders past and present.

The moral right of the author has been asserted.

For Hachette Livre (Marabout)
Proofreading: Emilie Collet
Layout: NoOok
Stylist: Sandra Mahut
Illustrations: Valentine Ferrandi

For Smith Street Books
Publisher: Paul McNally
Translation: Lucy Grant
Editor: Ariana Klepac
Production Manager: Aisling Coughlan
Proofreader: Pam Dunne

Printed & bound in China

Book 303
10 9 8 7 6 5 4 3 2 1